The Big Girls Club ^{SM}

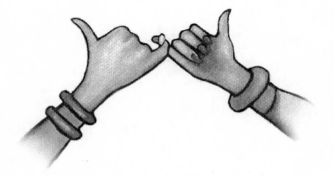

The Big Girls Club ℠

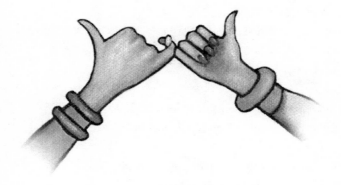

Little Girl Rules for the Big Girl Workplace

Judi Adams, MSEd, MFT

Gael B. Strack, JD

The Big Girls Club: Little Girl Rules for the Big Girl Workplace

Published by Wheatmark®
610 East Delano Street, Suite 104
Tucson, Arizona 85705 U.S.A.
www.wheatmark.com

International Standard Book Number: 978-1-60494-223-1
Library of Congress Control Number: 2008941249

Marketing by Lisé Markham and Kimberly Weisz
Cover illustration by Claudia Fernety

For more information on *The Big Girls Club*, or for online ordering and bulk discount information, please visit www.TheBigGirlsClub.org.

The concept of The Big Girls Club arose from our collective work experiences and our friendships with Teri and Debbi. We used these experiences and friendships to create stories illustrating the rules of The Big Girls Club. References to people, events, establishments, organizations, or locales were made to convey a sense of reality and authenticity and are used fictitiously. All other names (except for Teri and Debbi), characters, places and all dialogue and incidents portrayed in this book are the product of the authors' imaginations.

Contents

Acknowledgments

Writing this book was a labor of love and friendship. We first thank two favorite men in our lives: Jan Strack (Gael's husband) for having the courage to be our editor, the wisdom to say just enough, and the ability to make us better writers; and Carl Adams (Judi's husband) for being our main cheerleader. Over the course of the last year, we heard two things from Carl: *write* the book and *finish* the book. Thank you both.

We are grateful to family and friends who encouraged us, read the first drafts, and begged us to write more: Ken and Andréa Burtech, Debbie Diller, Joel Strack, Jearl O'Neal, Lisé Markham, Kimberly Weisz, Teri Barclay, Katie Sanford, Pat Gafford, Mary Lydon, Liz Shear, and Brian Haworth.

A special thanks to Dominic and Julie Burtech for sharing their beautiful boat with us. It was an inspirational place to put our thoughts on paper for the first time. We might have finished that day but for Judi's temperature of 105 and Gael's accidental plunge into the bay. Thanks, Judi, for hauling me out.

Preface

On a day fraught with turf issues, power struggles, and egos, Gael Strack and I threw up our hands and sought the refuge of an adult beverage—a temporary respite from the storm. We were exhausted, and we needed a time-out.

Gael, a talented and dynamic prosecutor from the San Diego City Attorney's Office, had been tapped to develop and direct a program that would eventually become the national and international model for delivering domestic violence services. My consulting firm, Adams & Adams, Inc., had been recruited to help develop and implement a five-year strategic plan to guide the Center's operations and growth. The workload was enormous, not only because we were starting from scratch, but also because the program was instantly successful. Women and children (and some men) were flocking to the Family Justice Center for help even before the doors were officially open. Gael and staff were simultaneously "building and flying" this brand new way of delivering services to victims of family violence.

A new way of doing business: the learning curve was steep. Fifty on- and off-site partners had to work together, some from agencies that had been competitors for decades. Staffing for the Center was largely volunteer. Just imagine having the bulk of your workforce comprised of volunteers! In addition, Gael had police officers, prosecutors, therapists, domestic violence advocates, chaplains, medical professionals, and interns all working in the same location, all with different philosophies, approaches, and workplace cultures. Compounding all this was intense public scrutiny. Everyone was interested in the Family Justice Center concept, some because they thought it was revolutionary, others because it represented change and potential competition for funding. Every day was twelve hours long. Workdays, weekends, and holidays ran into each other.

So, on this particularly difficult day, over our adult beverages, we reflected on the difficulties of building a team and trying to get everyone—mostly women—on the same page, working together and pushing toward the same end point. We talked about what it takes to create an environment where power and control are *not* the governing principles, where everyone can succeed, and where everyone gets a second or third chance, or has the option of leaving with grace and dignity.

We reflected on the fact that the opportunities and challenges at the Center were enormous, especially for women. This was new territory. Careers could be jump-started here. Today's work would become the high point of tomorrow's resume. From our vantage point it was clear that this new setting and environment called for different workplace rules. The autocratic top-down models didn't work here. There were very few bosses on site, no formal reporting relationships with the usual sets of incentives and consequences. We needed new styles of behavior for self-starters who had to be team players, new incentives for independent thinkers who had to be collaborative problem solvers, new rules for players who had to be dedicated to the same end point—a common good. We needed new models for working together without anyone being in charge.

Looking for relationship models that functioned well, our conversation segued to friendships and what makes them work. I told Gael about my best friend of thirty-plus years: how we met, and how we decided to become best friends.

"You *decided* to be best friends? How did you do that?"

"We just decided what the rules of our friendship would be and we shook on it."

"Really ... and how long have you been friends?"

"Since we were seventeen years old, and we've never had an argument."

Teri and I met in the summer of 1964. I didn't like her at first. Well, I did and I didn't. She was almost six feet tall with long silvery blonde hair, big blue eyes, a little nose, perfect teeth, and long legs. When I first saw her, it was at a girlfriend's apartment complex; Teri was sitting on a couch surrounded by gorgeous guys... seems that she had attracted every single available man in the apartment complex that Sunday. Who could compete with that?

Then she saw me in the doorway and said, "Come on in here. Who are you? Are you moving in? It'd be *great* to have another girl around here."

Hmmm. Maybe she wasn't so bad after all.

Later that evening, I was in my friend's apartment alone—she'd gone out with her boyfriend—and there was a knock at the front door. I hollered out, "Who's there?"

"It's me, Teri; can you come out and play?"

I opened the door. There stood Teri with a bottle of hair bleach and a comb. "Could you help me bleach my roots? I can't reach the back."

I burst out laughing. Something about being asked if I could come out and play *and* bleach her hair tickled me. It's like the big and little girl parts of ourselves recognized each other at exactly the same moment—we were on the road to becoming grown-ups, yet just a few steps away from being kids. I let her in and helped her bleach her hair as we listened to folk music and discussed boys, politics, and our dreams for the future.

As Teri prepared to leave, she turned to me, smiled, and said, "I think we're going to be best friends."

And, since we were about to pledge undying friendship for the rest of our lives, we decided we should figure out what it would take to stay best friends. Over that summer we took turns telling each other about what mattered, what we believed in, and what our bottom lines were. We agreed on the rules for our friendship—rules that nurtured us through our adolescence, marriages, divorces, liberation, and careers. Here are a few of our rules:

Never date each other's exes. This was our number one rule, a no-brainer. First it was just our respective ex-boyfriends. Later it included ex-husbands and ex-lovers. Our friendship would always be more important.

Always make room for each other. In that first meeting with Teri, when she welcomed me into the group of guys that were surrounding her, it turned out she was following what would become one of the most important rules of our friendship. We moved in different circles over the years; we had different interests and different friends. She was into the women's movement when I was into Young Republicans. She was into photography when I was into group therapy. Our friendship survived the decades and differences because we always made sure the other had a place in whatever world we were traveling.

One for all and all for one. No one could divide us ... ever. No splitting. Just don't even consider it. We wouldn't talk about each other with anyone else. We had each other's back.

Pinky finger swear. What was shared between us, stayed between us. We had complete confidence that our deepest darkest secrets would be safe, that our fears and worries could be shared—no judgments and no leaking. We would take them to our grave.

It's not your fault. Our friendship was the one place in the world where we were guaranteed the benefit of the doubt. Of course it was someone else's fault! Thing was, in that totally accepting environment we didn't need to be defensive. "Maybe it was my fault ..." "Well then, you must have had a good reason."

Share and share alike. If I needed a dollar and Teri had one, she'd let me have it. If I had a dress she needed for a party, I'd lend it to her. If she happened to ruin my dress by washing it when it should have been dry-cleaned, well, friendship was more important than a very expensive pure silk, hot pink minidress, size 11.

Baby Jane alert. Back in the '60s, Joan Crawford and Bette Davis, both aging movie stars, made a cult horror film called *What Ever Happened to Baby Jane?* Bette Davis played Baby Jane, a sixty-year-old child star grown old, who still ran around with her hair in long blond ringlets, mascara-ringed eyes, pinafore dresses, and Mary Jane shoes with ankle socks. In the middle of the movie, Teri turned to me and whispered, "When we get old, if you see me starting to look like that, dressing like a crazy old lady with big rouged cheeks and too much makeup … promise me you'll tell me? Just look at me and say, 'Baby Jane alert!' and I'll know. Tell me—don't let me walk around looking stupid with people talking about me."

Never trust women without female friends. It was actually Teri's mother who had said women who didn't like other women shouldn't be trusted. They didn't observe the unspoken rules of sisterhood; they would take up all the limelight, didn't share, and often complained, usually to guys, that those other women were jealous of them. Guys often felt sorry for them and believed that they were being picked on by mean girls. Teri said there was no way to win with those people; best to just step aside and give them wide berth.

As I finished the story, Gael and I looked at each other as if hit by a bolt of lightning. That was it! What we needed were rules of friendship for women in the workplace. What if we developed guidelines that would help us learn, develop, and grow at work, and at the same time help us stay friends? And what if these guidelines became the foundation of a club—the Big Girls Club—not a club of exclusion, but a club of inclusion, where the dues were mentoring and teamwork?

We began looking more closely at the difficulties

and successes we'd experienced in the workplace. We talked to other women we held in high esteem, who would definitely be classified as Big Girls, gathering their stories, experiences, challenges, fears, tears, and cheers, and along the way we found some answers. We discovered that on some level the rules were already there, often unspoken and certainly unnamed.

Gael: Judi, Judi, Judi. Remember, we also want to talk about men and tell our readers that we don't hate men. We actually love them and are married to two wonderful guys.

Even our male colleagues became excited when we talked about the Big Girls Club; they had their stories to tell. We discovered that men wanted to have great working relationships with women too! But most didn't have a clue about the intricacies of the unspoken rules of the Big Girls Club.

Note to the Reader

We knew writing this book together would test the validity of our own membership in the Big Girls Club. The fact that you are reading this is a testimony to successful application of the Big Girl rules to our own collaborative effort.

In the following chapters, we share some of our Big Girl stories and experiences with you, and we name the Big Girl rule that we identified within each story. We realized that the key to the Big Girls Club was our experiences with other women in the workplace. We knew we were on the right track because, when we shared our stories with others, we found that everyone had their own story to add.

You will identify with some of the stories, having had similar experiences. You will have your own stories to tell and will discover your own Big Girl rules along the way. We dedicate this book to all of you who are, or will soon become, members of the Big Girls Club.

Judi: Where do we start?

Gael: Let's begin with "Cross My Heart—Hope to Die," the story that officially launched the Big Girls Club.

Rule Number One

Cross My Heart—
Hope to Die

Jasmine

Jasmine offered to help. It was one of those totally whacked-out days when everyone was running fast and hard. I (Judi) was going to facilitate a big meeting with lots of participants and normally I hired someone from my pool of consultants to document the meeting for me so I could turn the notes into a final report. I hadn't hired anyone yet. I was busy making phone calls, looking for someone, when Jasmine came into my office. She said, "Instead of hiring someone, use me. I'd love to do this for you. I can do it on my own time and you can pay me. I'm good, I'm fast, and I'd love to learn from you. Let me help you."

"Are you sure? You have to capture what people actually say. You have to use our standardized format. You take the notes during the meeting and send them to me electronically within one week. Are you sure you have time to do this? I can send you a template so you can see what it should look like when it's done. But I need it back to me within a week."

"Yes, I'd love to do this. I can do this. I want to help you. I want to learn to do this."

Ahhhh.

She came to the meeting as promised, set up her laptop, gave me a big smile and a thumbs up, and I was off and running with the group. During a lull, I stopped to glance over her shoulder at her laptop screen; she wasn't typing into the template I'd sent her. I asked her about it. She looked up and smiled calmly at me. "I had trouble downloading your document. I'll do it this way and drop it into the template later. No problem ... this is a piece of cake, really."

Hmmm.

The meeting ended and I told her to call me if she needed help. Time passed. No contact from her. Mid-week, I e-mailed her. "How's the report going?"

"I'm really busy right now. I have to get back to you ... everyone is piling things on me right now. I can't talk."

Hmmm!

The end of the week came and went. I e-mailed her again. "Hey, I really need that report. How's it coming? Do you need help?"

"I'm so busy; you can't believe all the things that I

have to do. I'll have to get back to you. I'm working on the report. Just give me an extra day."

Uh oh!

Two more days passed. I stopped by her office. "Look, I have to have that report. Why don't you let me see what you have done?"

"Judi, I wish you would stop pressuring me. I have so much on my plate. I'm so busy. I'm exhausted. Everyone expects me to be at their beck and call. I am so overworked. Nobody helps me. Everyone dumps on me. I'll get this to you as soon as I can. I'm doing the best I can."

Grrrr.

And there I was, trapped. Somehow I had just become the ogre to this poor girl—someone who was, apparently, busier than any of the rest of us. My disappointment was twofold: one, I didn't get the work that was promised, and two, I really liked her and thought she was one of the Big Girls who kept their word and their cool. Then from somewhere inside, anger and frustration bubbled over. I blurted out, "Jasmine, you will never make it in the Big Girls Club!"

She looked stunned, as if I'd cursed her. "What's the Big Girls Club?" she asked anxiously.

Thinking fast on my feet, I began telling her about the unspoken rules that Gael and I had been discussing; the things that are never said, but are known by Big Girls; the opportunities that are directed toward some women and away from others; the knowing glances that are exchanged when decisions and assignments are being handed out.

What Jasmine said next was totally unexpected. I would never have guessed her response. She mulled over what I had said for a moment and then asked, "What do I have to do to join?" That's when the Big Girls Club was officially launched. I agreed to become Jasmine's Big Girl mentor, and later that night Gael and I decided we had to do more than just talk about what Big Girls should do. We had to start writing it down.

DISCUSSION

Gael: I remember that night. You called me and asked if I had two minutes. You were hot! I asked you how you felt about all this, what impact it was having on you.

Judi: That's right! I talked about how on one level— you know that little girl place inside, the one we all have—I wanted to respond to Jasmine's emotional outburst in kind: "How dare you. You promised me! You said you wanted to do this. How is this *my* fault?" But on another level, I was looking at her and thinking, "How in the world is this smart young woman going to make it if she behaves like this? She has no idea about the consequences of her behavior—how people will distance themselves from her and never tell her why."

Gael: And that was the first time we started asking the question, "What would a Big Girl do?"

What Would a Big Girl Do?

First, she would keep her promise! Jasmine broke the "cross your heart and hope to die" rule. She didn't get the work done and left me high and dry. She placed me in jeopardy. I was depending on her and others were depending on me. Second, a Big Girl would take responsibility. Instead, Jasmine became very emotional and blamed everyone but herself for not getting the work done. I ended up having to do the work myself— and I was working all night as it was.

What Was the Solution?

I decided to indoctrinate Jasmine into the Big Girls Club. I established a mentoring relationship with Jasmine and I shared the rules with her. I decided to mentor her because, not only was this a person I had to work with, I liked her. That was her saving grace. She was likable; not dependable, but likable. I could have walked away and never asked her to do anything for me again, but I hate working like that. I hate turning away and not giving a colleague a chance to step up to the plate. Besides, it's so much more fun to be friends.

Gael: Did that work?

Judi: "Yes, absolutely, even though it did happen again. Not with me, but another pressure-cooker situation with co-workers. Later, when she was debriefing with me, she paused and asked, "I wonder how a Big Girl would have handled it?" Then she took a deep breath and said she knew what she had to do. She went back in and cleaned it up herself. Took responsibility, made amends. That's progress. The Big Girls Club isn't about perfection. We all have little-girl lapses. We aren't looking for perfection, just progress.

Ultimately, Jasmine changed professions; she realized that the pressures she faced in her job didn't bring out the best in her and she wasn't doing the kind of work she really loved. That was another big step, making a career move to find something that better suited her talents and strengths. Today, she is very happy, has her own business and loves her life. She says she owes it all to "The Big Girls Club!"

The truth is, we owe a lot to Jasmine. It turned out that Jasmine actually helped us articulate some of the Big Girl rules. It confirmed for us that, just like when we were little girls on the playground, the rules helped make our friendships work. We still need them today; it's just that the playground has been replaced by the workplace. Here are some of the lessons we learned from the Jasmine story.

TAKE-HOME MESSAGES

- If you get the feeling that someone is not going to deliver, trust your instincts and give that person a graceful way to back out. Take back the assignment. Make other arrangements to have it done.

- Don't engage in or indulge emotional outbursts. It's hard to apply logic or reason to an emotionally charged situation. You can't argue with someone's feelings. You want to be able to address the behavior, not the emotion.

- If you are going to continue working with that person, take a break. Come back after emotions have cooled and have a discussion from a calmer, Big Girl perspective.

- Remember, there are over fifty ways to respond to any situation. Take a deep breath and think of healthy ways to respond. You have a choice.

- One of our personal favorites: use your sense of humor to deflect an icky situation.

- If you're not going to work with that person again, then you have other options. Don't say anything, let it go and move on. Or, give her a copy of this book; circle *this* chapter and hope for the best. At least you gave them something to think about.

- If you promise to do something, mean it and do it. Don't take on more than you can handle. There is no shame in knowing your limitations and setting healthy boundaries. It takes a Big Girl to admit it.

- If you find yourself in a situation where you're the one who can't deliver, tell someone and tell them early so they can make other arrangements. Remember the old cowboy saying: The easiest way to eat crow is while it's still warm. The colder it gets, the harder it is to swallow.

Gael, What's Next?

Judi, let's go to "Be Big." Jasmine reminds me of Wanda. Thanks to Wanda, I learned a valuable lesson when I was twenty years old. Wanda gave me a gift and neither of us knew it at the time.

Rule Number Two

Be Big

Wanda

My grandfather always told me, "Gael, when you're at work, you need to work hard. Stay out of the gossip and mind your own business."

So, there I was, twenty years old, working as a legal secretary to the senior counsel of a large legal firm in Los Angeles. I was hired the same day I applied. Down the hall, another twentysomething woman—tall, beautiful, exotic, and smart—was hired the same week. Wanda!

Wanda and I became fast friends. We worked in the same office. We came from similar modest backgrounds. We both wanted to become attorneys someday. We went on vacations and double dates together and went to school together. For two years we worked side by side. We both signed up for a paralegal course offered at Cal State, Los Angeles. We took the required classes together, studied together, drove together, and graduated together. Shortly thereafter, a position for a legal assistant opened. We both applied.

While waiting for the final decision, I continued to follow my grandfather's advice. I came in early and stayed late, worked through breaks and lunch. I was sure that everyone would notice how hard I was working and they would reward me for my efforts. Wanda, on the other hand, spent her breaks and lunches talking to people. She went out for drinks after work. Every time I looked up, wiping the sweat from my brow, there was Wanda, hanging out with somebody, chatting them up, and having a great time.

"Hah, that won't work!" I thought.

I was wrong. Wanda got the job. Like me, she had a plan. She was working hard at developing relationships, gathering information, learning the ropes, the secrets, and where the bodies were buried. She was networking.

Did my best friend screw me? Was Grandpa Joe wrong? I went home and cried. I threw a mini-tantrum. I was mad at Wanda. I was mad at myself. What hadn't I done? What did I miss? What happened to the rule that hard work paid off? I felt betrayed.

The experience of competing for a job with a close friend didn't feel good to me. I'm pretty certain it didn't feel so good to Wanda either. In my naïve world of "just work hard," I thought the great god of career advancement would reward me and give me what I deserved. I didn't want it to be a competition but it was. In those days, to get the upper hand, women were emulating male rules … the good-old-boys club. To get ahead, you needed to win over the minds, hearts, and eyes of the power brokers.

As crushed as I was to not get the job, in the end, what really hurt was the loss of my best friend, Wanda. As you may have guessed, my relationship with Wanda was never quite the same again. Eventually we drifted apart. She made new friends and I made new friends. I realized that not all friendships at work last forever. Sometimes, work friends are just that—work friends.

At first, my new rule was going to be "don't become close friends with people at work," but that's not right. Friendships will (and should) form in the workplace. Often our best friendships happen at work. That's where I met my husband. That's where I met Judi.

What worked for my grandfather in the 1940s, when—like many in his day—he worked as a laborer, wasn't going to work for me, a young woman pursuing a professional career in the 1980s. Relying on fierce de-termination and hard work, my grandfather emigrated from Cuba to New York, eventually opening the first Jewish deli in Los Angeles. But forty years later, in a work environment driven more by ideas and innova-tion than by persistence and sweat, different rules ap-plied.

What were these new rules? Obviously Wanda had figured out a few things (like networking), but what else did she know that I didn't? I needed someone, something, that would tell me the unwritten rules. I needed a rulebook for being a Big Girl.

DISCUSSION

Judi: Wow! It was bad enough to lose out on a job that you really wanted, but to lose it to a close friend—that must have been tough.

Gael: Oh it was. It took me a long time to process the emotions of that experience and accept its lessons. I kept trying to coach myself into being big, to let it go, to forget about it. But I never forgot it. In fact, just talking about it with you brings it all back as if it happened yesterday. Still, there were so many great gifts in that experience as well.

Judi: I know you wanted to write this book to help your daughter. What were the gifts? What is worth passing on to your daughter and future women in the workplace?

First, Be Big

I needed to be BIG, to immediately transform my negative energy into positive energy, to turn electrons into protons, to make lemonade out of lemons. Maybe it would have helped to talk to Wanda the minute the position was announced, acknowledging our mutual interest. Maybe I could have refocused the situation— from a winner-take-all competition to a win-win situation—by talking about what we'd do if one of us got the job. Maybe we could have thought about next steps and adopted a "rising tide lifts all boats" approach, outlining our plans for the future regardless of who got the job.

Yes, it would have been nice if we had done all that, but we didn't. So how could I have been BIG after the fact? I could have congratulated her (and really meant it), taken her out to lunch, or bought her an adult beverage, celebrated her success, and even asked her to share her networking tips with me so I too could figure out how to network like a pro.

Even if she didn't share, so what! She was playing by the rules at a time when women didn't share the rules with each other. It was still pretty much a man's world, and women were just starting to climb the corporate ladder. Once they got on, they played by the rule "I'm on board, bring up the ladder."

Second, Don't Take It Personally

At some point I entertained the thought that maybe Wanda had set out to screw me. I even began plotting to take her out, using Machiavellian rules of engagement. That's when I started taking it personally. I was having a tantrum.

Fortunately I was smart enough not to have a public tantrum. I just went home to fume and cry. Too often, I've seen women go after worthy opponents by bad-mouthing coworkers, undermining them, and splitting them into camps. In the long run, they only ruin their own reputation.

Hell, I was only twenty years old, a mere 106 pounds (I'd love to see that weight again). I should have gone out, had fun, and counted my blessings. As it turned out, I ended up getting an even better promotion within two months anyway.

Judi: Okay, Gael, let's get real here. Let's test it. Suppose we both got asked to apply for a job, a great big fat juicy important job, and let's say it had a lot of money attached, and an airplane. What should we do, based on your Wanda experience?

Gael: I know exactly what we would do. We'd both race to the phone to call each other and see who wanted the job . . . and if we both did, we'd talk about how we could use the opportunity to advance each other. Then we would agree on where to fly.

Judi: I love it. That works for me. In that scenario, we both win.

Gael: Big Girls helping each other succeed. I like it!

TAKE HOME MESSAGES

- Be willing to help your friend succeed. Her success doesn't diminish your worth and talents. Embracing the success of others is unifying and opens up opportunities that may otherwise be closed.

- On the other hand, go after the job if you want it. There is nothing wrong with professional competition; indeed, competition is what allows the right people to find the right position.

- Have an alternative strategy—be a negotiator. If your friend is advancing, think through how it could benefit you, and talk to her about it. That's just plain good sense. Maybe she can hire you as her number two if she gets the job.

- Burning bridges is rarely smart strategy. As my husband always says, you never know who you may end up working for.

- Look around. There are Big Girls everywhere. Ask them for their secrets. If you're not comfortable asking or they don't tell you, then watch and learn. Write down their common characteristics.

- Let it go. Don't badmouth Wanda. Be big.

- Moan if you have to, but only for two minutes. Even cry a little, but get over it.

- Learn from the experience.

- Read books. Learn the art of networking and also mentoring. Reach out to women and men whom you respect, and who might be willing to serve as your mentor with the goal of helping you grow professionally.

- Try to see unpleasant work experiences as an opportunity to improve yourself and grow. It's like the gift inside every box of Cracker Jacks.

What's Next?

Judi　　So where do we go from here? What's next on our storytelling agenda?

Gael   I'd like to hear more about your relationship
        with Teri and your rule, "There's Always Room
        for One More."

Rule Number Three

There's Always Room for One More

Evelyn

Judi: Gael, remember when I told you about the first time I met Teri, how she welcomed me into the group of guys who were surrounding her, and how she made room for me, made sure I was included? That turned out to be one of the most significant rules of our friendship.

For example, there was the year we worked as campaign volunteers for Goldwater's run for the presidency. I was late getting to campaign headquarters at the Ambassador Hotel in Los Angeles. When I walked in, Teri was being interviewed live by NBC. She saw me and said, "Wait! Here's my best friend, Judi. She knows everything about Goldwater. Ask her a question." The reporter loved it. He couldn't ask enough questions. He spent hours with us. Snippets of that interview, it turned out, played all over the local LA news that night. Fun! We were only eighteen years old and we'd already had our fifteen minutes of fame; I owed it all to my best friend, Teri.

Then there were all the times that Teri and I would go and listen to folk music at the Hollywood coffee houses, the 5th Estate, the Omnibus, and the Troubadour. I loved to get up on stage to sing and play my guitar. Teri loved to sing too, but didn't think she sang very well, and she had to be encouraged. So I would introduce her from the stage. "Meet my best friend Teri. She sings great harmony, but she doesn't know it. Would you help get her up here to sing with me?" People would cheer her on. Teri would just die, but she'd come on up and she'd sing with me. People loved it. Our fun was so contagious; folks could feel it. We were welcoming them into our world. We wanted them to have fun. There was room for everyone.

Gael: That's all well and good in a friendship, but what happens when girls don't make room for each other in the workplace? Aren't we supposed to strive to get ahead? That means there will be times that we will need to compete with each other.

Judi: Hmmm. I think that exclusion is one of the ways that we make situations unnecessarily competitive. Inclusion is a way that everyone can come out a winner, if we are willing to share. Case in point: do you remember the night I called while on the way home from the dinner with our friends from New York?

Dignitaries came in from all over the country for an important conference. We would be having a small dinner meeting the night before with two very important, high-powered women from New York. It was our first meet and greet. There was a lot riding on this dinner. First impressions counted. They wanted to get to know us and hear about our organization.

When I arrived at the restaurant, Evelyn (a co-worker on the project) was already there. She was standing in the very crowded lobby with our guests from New York, waiting for a table. They were deep in conversation. I squeezed in behind Evelyn, nudged her so she knew I was there, and waited for her to introduce me. But she didn't. She just continued talking ... all about herself. I waited. Minutes went by, and I still hadn't been introduced.

While I was trying to figure out what to do without being impolite, our two guests made eye contact and smiled at me—that provided me the opening I needed. I smiled and stuck my arm out over Evelyn's shoulder and offered my hand, sort of at a right angle. They reached out and touched my fingertips and mouthed "Nice to meet you" so as not to interrupt Evelyn's story.

Oh my God. Evelyn kept right on talking even after we were seated. I made attempts to open up the conversation and turn it to the topics we wanted to cover. Evelyn answered all questions and drew the conversation back to herself, her work on the project, her experiences. Another colleague joined us, bravely plunged in. She too was thwarted. You would have thought that Evelyn had singlehandedly developed and run the entire program.

Gael: I assume that at this point you wanted to drag Evelyn out to the parking lot to delicately "explain" the rules of the friendship?

Judi: You have no idea. Evelyn was cutting us all out of the conversation, grandstanding. We certainly weren't demonstrating good teamwork and collaboration, the hallmark of our program. And the longer I did nothing, the more pathetic we all looked. Our guests' eyes were glazing over. Their smiles were pained. They reached for their wine glasses and began glancing at their watches as the final dregs of energy left the table.

I decided that it was every woman for herself. I reached out to the guest nearest me, literally. I took her arm to get her attention and plunged in with a barrage of questions.

Wham. Evelyn tried to bring her back. "Judi, I was just explaining that ..."

Hah. I leaned forward in my chair and turned my back to Evelyn, blocking her from our guest's line of vision. "Please," I said to my guest, "you were saying?"

For a few minutes it was like a fencing match—joust and parry. In the end, I prevailed. You should have seen the relief spread across our guest's face. She began talking about her passions, hopes, and dreams for this project, why they had come out to meet with us. A real conversation started. I was able to draw in our other colleague. We got a three-way conversation going.

When I dared to glance down at the other end of the table, I saw that the other guest was gone, maybe to the parking lot to study the striping pattern or to the restroom to commit hara-kiri. Who knows? She'd managed to make her getaway. Evelyn was still talking, but now to the waiter. She was telling him in great detail about the terrible service she'd received at a nearby restaurant. He was casting his eyes around, desperately looking for an escape. He looked at me. I just looked away. He was on his own.

DISCUSSION

Gael: What does this have to do with competition and making room for everyone?

Judi: Evelyn didn't make room for anyone. This shouldn't have been a competitive situation, but Evelyn made it a monologue about herself to the point that our guests became uncomfortable. We almost lost the opportunity to discuss the new partnership. And it wasn't fun. These were influential women who valued time. While they wanted to get to know us on a personal level, they didn't come two thousand miles to spend an evening listening to one person drone on and on about herself.

What Were Your Solutions?

Judi: I first waited for a graceful way to break into the conversation. Ultimately, when that didn't work, I was forced to compete with my own team member. I refocused my attention to the task at hand—promoting the organization and establishing a working relationship with our guests from New York. I played *Risk*. I created an opportunity to jump into the conversation then hung onto it for dear life.

Gael: That's a great way to break into the conversation, but how did you deal with Evelyn after the fact?

Judi: Quite frankly, in this case, I didn't.

Gael: Why not? Why wouldn't a Big Girl approach work for Evelyn?

Judi: The Big Girl approach is not going to work
         with everyone. Some people will not want to
         change. There are some people who will not
         hear what you are saying no matter how loudly
         you speak. It might even make the situation
         worse. I had to be realistic. To maintain a pro-
         fessional working relationship with Evelyn,
         I focused on her strengths and set up strate-
         gies for myself to manage future engagements
         with her. I included her where her gifts would
         be helpful and avoided situations where she
         wouldn't be helpful.

TAKE-HOME MESSAGES

Gael: Okay, let's summarize. What recommendations
         do we have for Big Girls who want to make
         room for others at work?

- Before important meetings, have a discussion with
  members of your team about the purpose and desired outcomes.

- Assign tasks to team members that play to their
  strengths. Solicit their input and desired outcomes
  for the meeting. Agree to work together and set
  your own ground rules.

- Keep focused on the business at hand and try to figure out how to engage others in the conversation.

- Remember that it's not all about you. You don't have to do it all yourself.

- You win big points by praising the work of others on your team and making room for others in the conversation.

- People will trust you and return the favor.

- Beware the consequences of Evelyn-like behavior. Others may not want to play with you, include you in important meetings, or—gulp—invite you out to another dinner.

What's Next?

Gael: Let's move on to Sally now.

Judi: Okay ... I'll tell you Sally's story and then maybe together we can figure out all the important lessons that can be gleaned from that painful experience.

Rule Number Four

Be Nice—Play Fair

Sally

When "Sally" first joined our agency, a new child abuse treatment program in LA, everyone congratulated themselves for bringing her on board. She was exactly what the organization needed: the right degrees, good connections, a friendly personality, and a dry sense of humor with an edge. We were sure we'd hired the right person.

During the first year, Sally was getting things done and making things happen. She got along with coworkers and seemed happy to be part of the team. Oh, she might talk a little too much about *her* accomplishments, and she'd occasionally hint that this coworker or that colleague had dropped the ball, and that she'd needed to step in and save the day. But for the most part, everything seemed to be going smoothly enough. In hindsight, the clues were there. We had small uh-oh feelings (what Gael calls that little alarm that goes off somewhere deep inside—it's subtle and easy to over-look). Well, we minimized our feelings then; in retro-spect, a definite mistake.

As the second year began, we added staff. The new people were full of enthusiasm, fresh ideas, and sug-gestions about improving operations and expanding services. The monthly team meeting was the vehicle for discussing operations and problem solving.

During meetings, when staff presented on their projects, Sally would roll her eyes, start sidebar conver-sations with the person next to her, or interrupt to say, "I'm taking care of that," or "I told you to leave that to me, I'll get it fixed." If someone brought up a new idea, Sally would speak as the resident expert and present a dozen reasons why it couldn't be done. If someone dis-agreed with her, she would interrupt and accuse them of "not letting me finish."

Then Sally started showing up in a funky mood. You could feel it in the halls. She'd sit sullenly in her office with her door closed or come to a meeting and contribute nothing. Even her silence was noisy. Every-one knew she was unhappy about something. But if anyone tried to draw her out or include her, she'd refuse to respond or just get up and walk out.

The team began walking on eggshells, trying to work around her. People started running complaints up the chain of command. Special meetings would be held to work things out, essentially to deal with problems Sally was causing. But each effort was met with further negativity, hostility, and even insubordination. Sally would gossip. She'd walk right out of a meeting and into someone's office. She began openly pitting people against each other. She'd badmouth her coworkers, colleagues, clients, friends, partners, and eventually the boss. She totally broke ranks and pulled in colleagues from other agencies to tell them "her side of the story"—the story she was manufacturing. People took sides. Pro-Sally camps began to sprout. She'd trap people by swearing them to secrecy. They could only talk to her.

Morale took a downturn. More meetings were held. The human resources department was called in. It was never her fault. It was always someone else's. She was the one being wronged. People were against her. The facts, as Sally saw them, were very compelling; they supported her point of view completely.

Things became very muddled and confused. In the end, it was her long-suffering coworkers who finally broke the spell. They began talking among themselves, comparing notes and checking out the things she was telling them. As it became clear who and what had been causing the problems, they refused to cooperate with her gossiping. They were in open rebellion. They would avoid her like the plague. She eventually left the organization, but by the time she left, she had lost all credibility and all of her friendships. She drove everyone away.

DISCUSSION

Gael: As you told that story, I couldn't help but wonder, where was management, accountability? How could she get away with that behavior for so long?

Judi: Sally was very slippery. She was nice and sweet to the boss, gave the boss everything the boss asked for, obscuring a smoldering fire within the organization. It was hard to see through the haze. The boss was trying to play fair and not take sides.

What Would a Big Girl Do to Handle the Sallys of the World?

First off, Big Girls always play fair, regardless of whether they want to or not. Sally's violation was her complete and total focus on herself, her own needs, her own agenda, and her own viewpoint. She cared only for herself.

Big Girls also play nice. Sally wasn't nice. Her unwillingness to share credit for accomplishments, her hints that other people weren't doing their jobs, her "that won't work" attitude, all those behaviors stifled individual and team creativity. Her gossip and her negativity made her unapproachable and undermined teamwork and friendships. It drained energy and sapped possibilities.

Gael: Oh, Judi, I can feel your pain. Was it difficult to write about this?

Judi: I found that I couldn't just tell the story without reliving it. I had left over feelings from my interactions with Sally and was still frustrated that it took so long for her to be brought to reckoning. It was like post-traumatic stress.

An enormous amount of time and energy went into just trying to solve this one work situation. It was so complex! In the beginning we could all see her potential, we liked her, and we wanted to be friends with her. But as time progressed, we could also see the damage she was causing. Nothing we tried worked. Why couldn't we fix this? We were the professionals with all the answers.

In the end, the only solution was to terminate the relationship. It was painful to see the wake of destruction she left behind, the unfinished work, the things we discovered had never gotten done. We had to start over. Workloads were heavier for a while, but just like recovering from a bad case of the flu, day by day we started feeling better. Our confidence in ourselves and our purpose returned. Our spirits grew lighter. We were wiser and we were a team again.

What Were Some of the Big Girl Lessons We Learned from This Experience?

To quote you, Gael, "If your uh-oh alarm goes off, pay attention!" Negative people suck the fun and energy from the workplace, and sarcastic humor is a first hint. Remember how I said she had a sense of humor with an edge? That edge turned out to be a dagger.

Negativity is cancerous—it breeds in silence. When people speak up, the silence is broken.

What was all the negativity and conflict covering up? Well, it turned out that while Sally was so busy putting others down to make herself look better, she wasn't doing her job. She was diverting folks' attention away from the fact that she wasn't doing what she was supposed to do.

Not everyone cares about being big. When it came time to change and play by new rules with new people joining the team, Sally was given every opportunity to get on board and do things differently. But she couldn't or wouldn't make the adjustment. She continued to make things up to support her version of reality.

It can take busy bosses a while to see the behavior that coworkers experience every day. People like Sally, who are focused totally on themselves, can be seductive, smart, and hard to pin down. They can present themselves in many different ways, especially to different people. Sally was very good at presenting a positive, can-do face to her boss.

What Are Some Solutions?

Judi: Grandpa Joe's advice is still relevant. Avoid taking sides. Don't get caught up in the gossip. Stay focused on the work and keep a positive attitude. Even though we had a tough time going through this, ultimately it was our focus that led to the right outcome.

TAKE-HOME MESSAGES

Gael:　Time to summarize. There's a lot to be learned from this story. What recommendations do we have that can help us be Big Girls?

- Stay positive and hopeful at work. Don't indulge in negative thinking—your own or anyone else's. The truth is that there are many different ways to do things. If new ideas or suggestions are repeatedly met with "That won't work," go ahead and ask why not, but don't forget to ask what they think *will* work.

- No dumping and running allowed. If someone keeps showing up in your office to complain about work problems, ask them to come up with a positive solution.

- Warning: misery loves company. Watch out for predators who will suck you into the muck; they stalk and recruit. Be careful. You have a bad day and a weak moment and before you know it, you get drawn in and can't get out. Don't indulge it.

- Never let anyone walk into your office and gossip about others, ever. Don't badmouth *anyone* at work. People will talk, and eventually what you said will get out and be traced back to you. Being a gossip can ruin reputations and block career advancement. And remember, hurt people hurt other people.

• Negative energy is not acceptable. Approach challenges with a positive attitude: accepting, not frustrated; open-minded and interested in problem-solving, not blaming or avoiding.

• Make it a policy not to talk about personal matters at work. Blue moods, bad marriages, family problems—everybody has them, but keep them out of the workplace. Have good resources outside of work to refer to when you help.

• Stay focused on the mission, its purpose, and the good working order of the team.

• If you or someone you know struggles with these issues, we advise getting help outside the organization. Find somebody you trust, somebody who understands you and can help you see things from a different perspective. The ten thousand-foot view is often the best place to start.

• If you are the boss, listen to your employees. If you are getting multiple complaints from multiple sources about a certain employee, listen and investigate. Your first instinct might be to doubt the stories because you haven't seen or experienced the bad behavior firsthand, but that doesn't mean it isn't happening.

Next?

Gael: Okay, Judi. Thanks for going through this again. How about you pick the next story?

Judi: Let's move on to something a little lighter. I'd like to tell you the story about Candy and the Baby Jane alert rule.

Rule Number Five

The Baby Jane Alert

Candy

When Candy got the job in the nursing office at the Good Samaritan Hospital, she was twentysomething, and she had two very little boys and an ex-husband who was well on the road to alcoholism. She'd started out as a file clerk in radiology and six months later was promoted to project secretary in the nursing office. Even though she didn't type very well, she got the job because people liked her a lot; she was very empathetic and a good listener—just a great people person.

One of her new responsibilities was the "Book of the Dead." When someone died in the hospital, their belongings were sent up to the nursing office and the body was sent down to the morgue in the basement. First thing every morning, Candy would come in and sort through these belongings, listing the items in the Book of the Dead. Then Candy would call the relatives, ask them to come by and pick up the belongings, have them sign the book, and make plans for the removal of the body from the morgue.

Sometimes, there was no next of kin to call. The patients died alone and Candy would have to go through their belongings, searching pockets, wallets, and old papers, trying to find a distant relative or old friend to come and claim the belongings and make arrangements for burial. As you might imagine, handling the Book of the Dead was the least favorite job among the rest of the nursing office staff.

Candy didn't love the idea of working with the belongings of the deceased either. It made her sad and it was rather morbid. However, the job paid a little more and her childcare costs, rent, and groceries had taken the bulk of her old paycheck; she had no surplus at the end of the month. Every bit helped.

And there was some good news. Now Candy could wear a uniform. That eliminated the struggle of trying to figure out what to wear every day. The bad news was that, on her income, uniforms were a luxury and she only had two. Since she didn't have a washer and dryer, she'd wash them out in the kitchen sink and hang them in the bathroom to dry. In the morning, she would hurriedly iron the one she was going to wear that day.

Those two uniforms became the bane of her existence. They were plain white and lost their shape after a few washings. When she added bleach to get out stains they turned a sort of yellowish gray. They wrinkled easily and, because they were polyester, which doesn't breathe well, they trapped body odor. The hospital was old and the air conditioner in the nursing office lacked conviction. So, after days of running up and down the back stairs of the hospital to collect belongings from the morgue, sorting through old clothes, suitcases, and papers, Candy's uniforms began to emit a sort of sour-damp odor that didn't wash out and, over time, permeated her office.

This didn't go unnoticed. But nobody wanted to say anything to her—not her supervisor and not the dozens of nurses who were in and out of the office every day. No one wanted to tell this good-intentioned, well-liked, hard-working young woman that she had a hygiene problem. They certainly didn't want to lose her and nobody wanted to get stuck with the Book of the Dead. So instead they just made comments to each other. They cracked little jokes and kicked around suggestions: "Just put a bottle of deodorant on her desk." "Buy her some perfume." "Leave her an anonymous note."

Finally, Candy's supervisor called the human resources director and they discussed the best way to handle the awkward situation. They came up with a plan. They would call her in and review the hospital's dress code with her. That was it. She was in violation of the dress code! Hopefully, that would take care of it.

But before the HR plan could be put into place, something else happened. Candy came to work in a brand new baby blue uniform. The next day she showed up in another—light yellow this time—and on the following day, a soft pale green one. For a whole week, she came in with a new uniform every day: clean, crisp, and wrinkle free. The odor problem was gone and the appearance problem was solved. Whew. Everyone was happy. No one had to talk to Candy.

DISCUSSION

Gael: Why did you call this chapter "Baby Jane Alert"?

Judi: Remember the story I mentioned in our preface—the one about *What Ever Happened to Baby Jane*? It was a blockbuster hit. The main character, a mean old woman who had been a child star called Baby Jane, continued to keep her hair in long ringlets and wore pinafore dresses and patent leather Mary Jane shoes complete with ankle socks. It was my best friend who came up with the "Baby Jane alert" rule. At the core of the rule was this: if you care about me, you'll tell me if I am doing something embarrassing or harmful to myself. Candy needed a Big Girl to befriend her.

What Should the Big Girls at the Hospital Have Done to Help Candy?

Candy needed a gentle Baby Jane Alert, but her co-workers in the nursing office didn't know how to deliver it.

Luckily, a Big Girl did emerge: a file clerk from HR. Her name was Betty. She got wind of HR's intervention plan, thought it was bureaucratic overkill, and figured it probably wouldn't work. She knew Candy slightly and liked her well enough. She suspected Candy didn't have a clue that people were discussing her behind closed doors.

So Betty took matters into her own hands and asked Candy out to lunch. Betty leveled with her about what was going on, but gently. She told her all the good things people said about her and how everyone thought she was doing a great job. Then she talked about how Candy's appearance was being scrutinized in a new light now that she was out in the public eye.

And then she shut up and listened while Candy explained her lean circumstances. Betty got it. It wasn't that Candy didn't care; she was living hand to mouth. She needed some help. Betty helped Candy find a wholesale uniform store—one that did a lot of business with hospital staff and was willing to extend credit.

What Lessons Did You Learn from This Experience?

I love Candy's feisty coworker, Betty. Good for her for stepping up and taking on the problem. Betty was the epitome of a Big Girl. The advice probably went down more smoothly coming from Betty because she and Candy were peers. It would be great if every workplace had a Big Girl like Betty and a rule like the Baby Jane alert.

Real help is based on a clear understanding of real need. Betty did a great job delivering the Baby Jane alert to Candy. She praised her, pointed out her gifts, and reassured her that her coworkers valued her. Then she talked about the problem and took the time to carefully listen and find out the facts. Finally, she helped Candy resolve the issue.

People are reluctant to talk about personal issues, but it is important to deal with them sooner rather than later. If it gets into the gossip mill, it can end up causing a great deal of pain and embarrassment.

It's very difficult to bring up sensitive issues when there hasn't been any discussion about how to do it. HR policies are not the same as coworkers taking it upon themselves to develop their own Baby Jane alert system.

TAKE HOME MESSAGES

Gael: Let's summarize the key points in this story.

- Don't take a pass on a personal issue. You may be the one person who can do something about it.

- Make a rule like the Baby Jane alert with your colleagues and friends. Have a discussion with co-workers about how they'd want to be dealt with if a personal issue became a problem in the workplace.

- If you are the one addressing the problem, first talk about strengths and positives and how much the colleague is valued. It's easier to hear bad news if we are reassured of our worth first.

- Be willing to listen, analyze, and problem-solve.

- Trust your instincts, absolutely. If your gut says "uh-oh," then take some time and think it over before you make the intervention.

What's Next?

Judi: I love the Candy story. It's such a great example of a Big Girl stepping up to the plate.

Gael: I agree. And Candy, like Jasmine, was likable.
       Maybe it's time for the story "Beware of Wom-
       en Without Female Friends." Scarlett was quite
       the opposite of Jasmine and Candy.

Rule Number Six

Beware of Women Without Female Friends

Scarlett

The male board president recruited and lobbied the executive director to hire Scarlett to be the new fund-raiser for our small social service agency. "She's great! She's exactly what we need. She has good connections and we don't have any time to waste."

And so it came to pass that Scarlett joined our little team and began planning her first big event. "We'll have a holiday party on Rodeo Drive and get it catered by the chefs from the Beverly Hills Hotel. We'll have an auction and raffle off crystal ornaments, get a quartet from the symphony to come and play holiday music; people will buy tickets and bring presents for the children. We'll have imported champagne. It'll be fun; everyone will come and we'll raise lots of money."

She tossed her long fiery red hair and gracefully swept her tiny hand across the horizon of the boardroom as she described her vision. We could all see it. Wonderful! A great event! She was obviously very connected. What a coup. Board members congratulated the president. He was smiling from ear to ear. She was saying exactly what he wanted to hear. She was playing him like a violin. She went to work.

Scarlett moved like a house on fire. She was a whirlwind of activity. Everyone was mesmerized by her energy. She met with printers and caterers and the hotel's hospitality staff. She ordered invitations and bought exclusive mailing lists. She had the bills sent to accounting.

The board president was happy. Things were getting done.

Scarlett was totally charming with everyone—especially the president. However, when the executive director asked her for the third time to come up with a budget for her big event and to get prior approval for purchases, Scarlett went straight to the president to complain. "She [the executive director] doesn't support me. She criticizes everything I try to do. She wants to control my every move. I can't work like this. My friends and all my connections are important people. I need to be able to move fast and get decisions made if they're going to help us. She doesn't realize that you have to spend money to make money. She is going to ruin this event for you!"

The executive director, unable to get Scarlett to cooperate, also went to the president. She voiced her concerns about Scarlett's extravagance and behavior. "Scarlett's a lovely person, but she doesn't seem to want to cooperate with me. She doesn't give me the things I ask for, won't take direction. She's spending a lot of money for this event. She's vague about details and no funding is coming in yet. I'm not seeing a lot of follow-through. I think we may have a problem here."

The president listened and said, "Look, we all need to just get along. You're overreacting. Scarlett's fine. You're being a little hard on her. Just give her what she needs—she knows what she's doing. She's a professional and that's why we hired her. We all need to support her. Try to relax. Tell you what: I'll work with Scarlett on this project. You run the agency. Everything will work out fine."

Six months later, the party was every bit as beautiful as Scarlett had promised. The crystal ornaments shimmered in their midnight blue display boxes on the auction tables. Champagne flutes sparkled against the backdrop of holiday lights and platters of gourmet food were piled high on tables dressed in gold, red, and purple. Over the top of it all, tinkling silver bells and sweet violins played on.

The party went off without a hitch except for one

thing: there was almost nobody there to see it. Only seventy-five people attended; we had expected four hundred. The event raised absolutely no money and it cost a small fortune. All those key items—food, hotel, chef, ornaments, champagne—all had to be paid for. Scarlett's plan had been to pay for it out of the proceeds from ticket sales . . . only there weren't any sales.

Scarlett defended her position to the board president vehemently. "You have to spend money to make money. Next time will be better. We got a lot of good publicity out of this and a lot of good will. This is not *my* fault; the executive director doesn't support me. I couldn't get any cooperation from her. She wouldn't give me the help I needed. She didn't believe in my event—was so negative towards me. She doesn't have a clue about what it takes to raise really big money. She doesn't have your vision." The president believed her.

It got worse. For the next six months, Scarlett moved fund-raising committee meetings off-site. If the executive director said she was coming, suddenly the meeting date would be rescheduled. Scarlett brought in some friends to join the board, all men. "These are important people with a great deal of wealth. They have deep connections. We're lucky they're willing to serve on the board." The other members were elated. This was exactly what they needed—a prestigious, moneyed board that could help with the fund-raising.

The president was very happy indeed.

Scarlett began planning her next event, a summer

fling, this time at a board member's estate in Beverly Hills. "White tents out on the lawn. Everyone will dress in summer whites … we'll have the best restaurants cater picnic baskets. Guests will bid on them. We will set up white wicker furniture out under all the trees and have croquet laid out on the lawn and icy fountains of sparkling white wines. Then, at sunset, we will have a concert outdoors, under the trees, while waiters serve coffees and aperitifs and gourmet desserts. And I have three sponsors already. The publicity will be fantastic. Everyone will want to come. Your summer event will be the social event of the season."

Scarlett began drawing large amounts of cash to reserve the tents and hire the musicians. The executive director became frantic watching the agency's coffers being drained. Where was the oversight? Who was watching Scarlett's spending? This time, the executive director wasn't the only one who saw the lavish spending. Other board members saw it too and they began asking questions. Immediately, Scarlett went into defense mode and told everyone, "Don't worry, we have underwriters, and ticket sales will easily cover the costs."

Scarlett had strategically invested her time with the men on the board, and it was no surprise that board members started taking sides. As the men saw it, the real problem was two female employees who simply couldn't get along with each other—basically a catfight. The women on the board saw things differently. Despite the tension in the air and closed-door discussions, there was no resolution. The board ultimately advised the executive director to leave Scarlett alone, and the event went on as planned with no effective oversight or controls.

The next event followed the same pattern. In the end the executive director gave up and quit.

Two years later, Scarlett left too. She stated that she was moving on to raise funds for a foundation. No one knows what really happened. But by the time she left, the damage had been done. There were hurt feelings everywhere. Friendships ended and board members resigned.

DISCUSSION

Gael:　Judi, what was going on with the staff during this time?

Judi:　Staff watched it all from a distance. Scarlett had the ear of the board president and she carefully protected her relationship with him. No one could penetrate it. She was impervious. In the meantime, she was pretty awful to all of the women on the staff—condescending, demanding, and abrupt. What would be the point of complaining, and to whom? Everyone saw how she'd driven out the executive director. She simply would have taken one of us out too. She was deadly.

Gael: Did the executive director ever try to work it out with Scarlett, maybe try to find a middle ground to work together?

Judi: Many times. At first, the executive director and Scarlett met regularly. Monthly meetings were set but they were also routinely cancelled. When problems came up, the executive director would contact Scarlett directly. Promises were made to do better or meet more frequently. But these promises were also broken. By the time the executive director took her concerns to the president, it was too late. Scarlett had already laid the defensive groundwork with him. She went behind the executive director's back and over her head. Eventually, the executive director gave up.

Gael: Why did you call this chapter "Beware of Women Without Female Friends"?

Judi: When you and I have talked about this rule with other women, they instantly knew what we were talking about. They all knew someone who fit that description. Take your daughter, for instance. You told me you mentioned this rule to Samantha and she said, "Oh, I know. Those are the girls who break plans with you when a boy calls. They put boys first and they take up all the attention."

A good fictional example might be Scarlett O'Hara in *Gone with the Wind*. She was the firstborn, and her special relationship with her father set her apart from her sisters and her mother. In Scarlett O'Hara's society, men wore the pants and held the power. Secure in her role as her father's favorite, she did what she wanted. She wanted what men had: choice, power, freedom, and money. She had no respect for women and saw them as holding her back with their rules—had actual distain for them—and saw them as weak. She manipulated men to get what she wanted; married her first husband for revenge, not caring that he had been pledged to another; and later married again—this time her sister's beau to get his money. And she had an ongoing emotional affair with the husband of the one woman who truly loved her.

Other women didn't like her and for good reason. She didn't like them. Made fun of them. Wasn't open to having relationships with them. She didn't play by their rules. She was calculatingly seductive. She formed no female alliances and took what she wanted. She didn't need girlfriends—she had dozens of beaus and was always the center of attention, always getting what she wanted.

What Should a Big Girl Do When Faced with a Scarlett?

If you spot a Scarlett at work, run. Avoid working with her if you can. Our Scarlett didn't follow *any* rules. She didn't follow the leader. She never acknowledged the executive director as her boss. Why should she? She had the board president under her spell.

If anyone disagreed with her, she was ruthless in her response. She shamelessly badmouthed the executive director up the chain of command to get her way. When that didn't work, she played the "she's being mean to me" card with the president. She diverted attention away from the real problem, cast herself as a victim, and made her female boss out to be the bad guy. This diversion trivialized the real issues and activated the long-standing myth that women can't get along with each other. Eventually, Scarlett was instrumental in getting rid of the executive director. She didn't play nice or fair and will never play nice or fair.

If you can't avoid her, set boundaries and stick to your guns. The executive director failed to do this, giving up her leadership role when she allowed the president to take responsibility for supervising Scarlett. She didn't stand up for herself and protest the president's inappropriate interference in agency operations, and she didn't challenge the clichéd interpretations that "women just can't get along" and "it's just a catfight."

TAKE-HOME MESSAGES

- If you have to work with a Scarlett, be very clear about roles. Make sure your roles and responsibilities are clearly documented. She will try to wiggle out of meetings, rules, and reporting requirements. Stand your ground.

- Be careful if she tries to pull you into her drama. She may try to get close to you and share confidences in an effort to win you over. Don't misconstrue that as friendship. It's more than likely a means to a desired outcome—hers!

- If you are in charge, don't abdicate your position. You don't want to toss aside your authority and responsibility when the going gets tough. If someone is making a move on your position, stand your ground. Make noise if you are being violated.

- Be willing to face difficult situations. Don't try to sidestep conflict and disagreement—they are an inevitable part of the workplace. It's how you deal with them, and when, that counts. It can be uncomfortable, so talking about how to deal with problems before they occur can help. If you need further help, find another Big Girl to talk to.

- Reject the notion that women don't get along with each other because they are women. Big Girls cannot allow a workplace problem to be framed as "women just can't get along." It's demeaning and undermines the credibility and value of the women involved.

- Take the time and make the effort to clearly articulate the problem. Sometimes we intuitively know that a problem exists, but we don't have the business language to describe it and we fall back on personal words and emotions to make a point. Having the right words brings courage and confidence.

Some advice if you are a woman who doesn't have any female friends...

- Read *Gone with the Wind*. In the end, Scarlett is all alone.

Next Steps

Judi: That was my not-so-happy-ending story. Your turn.

Gael: Well, I guess I'd better talk about Gina. Her story is called "Kiss and Make Up."

Rule Number Seven

Kiss and Make Up

Gina

Gina was a colleague and a friend. She was part of our Big Girls club at work, although we didn't call it the Big Girls Club then. We were just a group of young women who all worked hard and had our sights set on advancement. We were helping each other to get ahead and we were having fun being friends. Gina had a long-term relationship with a man named Tony. He had been her first and only boyfriend since the age of sixteen, and Gina was now in her early twenties. Although Gina would complain about Tony from time to time, all of us thought they were sure to get married.

Then one day, during lunch, she told all of us that she had broken up with Tony. It was over. She'd caught him cheating. We immediately circled the wagons and went into support mode. We highlighted his many personality flaws, using colorful adjectives and adverbs, and generally disparaged everything we imagined may have been associated with him, including all his relations, past, present and future.

How could someone do this to our friend? Especially Gina. She was so very loyal. She really loved Tony and wanted to get married. To get her back into the swing of things, we agreed to go out for drinks at singles bars. We tried to identify men to set her up with. Well, Gina was very smart and attractive. It didn't take long for men to know she was available and they came calling. Gina was excited about all the attention. Although she was sad and in pain over the breakup, she was holding up rather well and liking her new life as a single woman; she liked dating men, lots of men.

At first, no one thought twice about anything. "Good for her. Let her go out and get it out of her system. That will teach Tony a lesson." In fact, we enjoyed the stories Gina would tell us every Monday morning about her dates and the men in her life. The problem was that she would tell others around the office too. It didn't take long for her social life to become a source of gossip; her dates became sordid escapades.

One day while we were all waiting for Gina to join us for lunch, one of the women in our circle of Big Girls mentioned that she was concerned about all the gossip going around at work. She wondered whether we should tell Gina what folks were saying about her and whether we should suggest that she be more discreet about her storytelling.

Everyone had a different opinion. Some said, "Yes,

she's our friend. If I knew people were talking about me like that, I would want to know." Another woman said, "No way. They're just **jealous** of the fun she's having. Leave it alone; it will **pass**." At the time, we left it alone, thinking it would pass. But it didn't. It got worse, and as far as we could tell Gina was clueless. I even had a few guy friends take me aside to say something about her. That was it. Finally, we agreed that Gina had the right to know.

Somehow I was elected to be the one to tell her. I was closer to her, and everyone said she would take it best from me. They said I had "a nice way of delivering bad news." In other words, I was the sucker. I gave it a lot of thought—when I would mention it; how I would tell her how much we cared for her; how, because we cared for her, we felt she would want to hear it from us.

Judi: What did you say? This must have been very difficult.

Gael: It didn't go well, certainly not as planned. I tried to talk to her in a private place. I tried to tell Gina how much I cared for her and admired her. I tried to tell her that based on our friendship and the special place in my heart that I had for her, I needed to share with her what people were saying about her.

But as soon I said, "I need to share what others have been saying about you," her expression and body language immediately changed. My heart sank. At that moment I realized I (we) had made a horrible mistake. I should have just kept my big (although sincere) mouth shut. Gina demanded to know what people were saying and who said what. She also wanted to know if the other girls knew I was talking to her about this. I explained everything to her. I came completely clean. The conversation ended after a few minutes, but it felt like hours.

Gina was deeply offended, wounded, and upset. I'm not sure if she was upset because she thought we judged her, because we hadn't said something sooner, or because it required a group decision to reach the decision that I would speak to her on behalf of the girls. Regardless of the reason, she proceeded to tear into me and also told me what she thought of the other members of our group. It was not pretty. She said we were not good friends at all. Good friends would not do what we had just done.

I repeatedly apologized to Gina. I tried to explain over and over again our good intentions and rationale for not having told her sooner and our anguished deliberations over whether we should say anything at all. I told her we all cared about her deeply and valued her friendship.

I didn't sleep that night. I decided to let things cool down and try again. The next day I called Gina on the phone to ask her out to lunch. She hung up on me. I was stunned. Whatever happened to forgive and forget? What about kiss and make up? We had been close friends for the last three years. Was Gina really going to throw away that friendship after one misunderstanding? Was our relationship that fragile? Was there nothing that I could do to make it better?

Later that day, I decided to relay my conversation with Gina to the rest of the group. None of us knew how to react. We were all trying to help but now we were bad and evil girlfriends.

DISCUSSION

Judi: This is a very sad story. How did this end? Did you get it fixed?

Gael: Gina never talked to us again. She distanced
        herself from all of us and eventually left the
        company without looking back.

Judi: Did you talk about what happened with the
        other women in your group?

Gael: Yes. We were equally surprised and stunned by
        her reaction. We never imagined she would re-
        spond in that way, just as we did not anticipate
        that in trying to be a good friend we would lose
        a good friend. It had a profound impact on all
        of us. Without knowing it at the time, I think
        the rule "kiss and make up" started that day.
        Never again did we allow conflicts to get in our
        way. The rest of us remain friends to this very
        day.

Judi: Could you say a little more about the "kiss and
        make up" rule? How does it apply to this sto-
        ry?

Gael: It's just like when we were kids. I remember
        fighting with my brother Dominic—and we
        had some pretty good fights. My mother would
        always say, You don't want to fight with your
        brother. You love each other. You need each
        other and you're going to need each other even
        more as you grow up. It's important that you

two learn how to get along, forgive and forget. I want both of you to go to your room (we shared a room together), talk about it, and make up. I don't want you to come out until you have kissed and made up. You know, I hated it when she said that, but she was right. I didn't want to stay mad at my brother. I loved him and I wanted to go back to playing with him as soon as possible. Or maybe we *both* just wanted to go back outside and play.

And that's what I wanted with Gina. I didn't want to her to be mad at me. I liked Gina and I wanted to go back to being friends. But we didn't or couldn't. This is a difference between men and women. For some reason—and I hate even saying this out loud—it seems men can have the fiercest disagreement, call each other impolite names, and then the next day it's like nothing happened. They continue exactly where they left off before the disagreement. Huh? How does that work? More often than not, it doesn't seem to happen with women.

What Did You Learn?

Judi: If you could go back in time, would you do things differently?

Gael: Knowing now what I didn't know then, I
would have established rules of the friendship.
My girlfriends and I should have asked her and
each other whether we wanted to be told something we didn't want to hear, and if we did,
how we wanted to be told. Then again, maybe
we should have taken a page out of the "Guys
Club" and either said nothing at all or made
it more of a passing comment, leaving enough
hints for Gina to figure out for herself.

TAKE-HOME MESSAGES

What should a Big Girl do when she has to share
bad news?

- Before you deliver it, ask your friend if she wants
  to hear it.

- If she says no, respect her decision.

- If she says yes, ask her how she wants to hear the
  bad news.

- Practice the two-minute rule. Say whatever you have
  to say within two minutes. Say it once. No need to
  repeat the message. Bad news is always heard the
  first time.

- Say it with respect, kindness, and love.

- If things don't go well, don't share the conversation with others.

- Don't try to get other colleagues at work or friends to take sides.

   What could a Big Girl do when she has to hear bad news?

- Be big when people who care about you try to tell you something you may not want to hear.

- Try to hear the message without taking it personally.

- If you do get upset about it, say what is bothering you and why. Do it briefly. Say what you have to say in two minutes. Don't repeat yourself over and over again.

- Hurt people hurt people. Try not to hurt your friend. Resist the powerful temptation to retaliate.

- Direct your comments at the behavior, not at the person.

- If your friend is in the wrong, be willing to accept a sincere apology; forgive and forget.

- If you accept the apology, really accept the apology.

- Let it go. Delete. Delete. Delete it forever.

RULE NUMBER EIGHT

Pinky Finger Swear

Keri

I (Gael) had just been added to an e-mail list of national policy makers. As a new board member, I began receiving e-mails from other board members about a pending proposal the board would soon be considering. There was one particular proposal that was generating a lot of interest—it concerned legislation pending in DC. In fact, the e-mails were downright heated. Professionals in the field were hotly debating this new legislation. There were strong, compelling, and passionate arguments on both sides. Some of the members of the board I had joined opposed the pending legislation. The issue directly impacted policy that my friend Keri—who was not a board member—and I were separately working on.

Thinking I could help bring both sides closer together on the issue, I forwarded one of those e-mails to my friend Keri, who was one of the proponents and leaders of the bill. Based on the messages I had seen so far, it was clear it was going to be a tough road ahead for my friend; she would need to answer many questions and overcome numerous concerns. She would also need to do a lot of educating to win the support of my new board.

Because I also supported the bill and saw its merits, I had decided to share the e-mail with Keri in order to help her understand the concerns that others were expressing. If she had this information, I thought, she could use it in a sensitive, positive, and thoughtful way. I told her the message was for her eyes only. She promised to keep it confidential. Since Keri was a woman of her word, I didn't think twice about it. It was as good as a pinky finger swear... well, so I thought.

Later that month, I had the opportunity to attend my first board meeting with this organization. I arrived early. I was excited and honored that I had been asked to join them as a board member. Their mission was important. The other members were powerful, highly respected women from across the nation. I had heard about their work and their reputations for years. I was finally going to get a chance to meet them. As I walked into the meeting room, someone from the organization was already there, getting ready for the meeting. Caterers were bringing in delicious treats and hot coffee. I looked at the big mahogany table and quickly saw that name tags and binders were already being arranged and placed on the table. I saw my name—with a handwritten note from the president—welcoming me to my first meeting. Quite frankly, I was thrilled!

Then I saw the vice president enter the room. She seemed upset about something. She had a brief conversation with the board president. I couldn't help but overhear the president say we would add "it" to the agenda. "It" was to be immediately discussed at the meeting.

When the rest of the group arrived, the president called the meeting to order. She asked everyone to introduce themselves and share a little bit about themselves and their organization. Wow. They were definitely an impressive group of smart, articulate, and committed women, just the group I wanted to be associated with. Everyone was happy to be there. I had even forgotten about the short exchange about "it" between the president and the vice president.

Then, the president's tone changed from warm and friendly to ominous and serious. She announced that something had come to her attention that she felt needed to be addressed immediately. The room went uncomfortably silent. The floor was given to the vice president, who was clearly not happy. She said that someone from our board was sharing e-mails with an individual who had a position on the proposed legislation that conflicted with what she believed the majority of the board wanted. She had been in a meeting, trying to reach a resolution on the pending bill when, right in the middle of the meeting and in direct response to one of her arguments, Keri Smith challenged her and said she wasn't representing the viewpoint of the entire board. The vice president went on to explain—much to my horror—that Keri stated she'd been receiving messages from board members.

Everyone in the room gasped. They were clearly outraged. Someone called out, "Who was it? How many board members are involved? We need to know!" This was followed by outcries. Loud comments about "betrayal" and "enemies amongst us" volleyed back and forth across the room as the situation reached crisis proportions. They wanted answers. They wanted heads to roll. Everyone started looking around the room, as if a scarlet letter would be written on the faces of the guilty or a neon sign would be flashing over people's heads—"Guilty! Guilty! Guilty!" I was surprised that they couldn't see it over my head. My heart was beating so fast I thought I would faint.

After the initial shock, some members began questioning the vice president in great detail in order to get to the bottom of it and find out who the culprit or culprits were. She didn't know—Keri had refused to disclose her source. (Whew. I breathed a huge sigh of relief.) Nevertheless, my heart sank. I knew immediately that my friend had shared the substance of the e-mail I had forwarded to her, and it was only a matter of time before this very sharp group of women figured it out how that e-mail had found its way to Keri.

DISCUSSION

Judi: Oh my gosh! What were you thinking?

Gael: Judi, I was just sick to my stomach. Initially, I froze. I didn't know what to do. Fortunately, the look of shock of my face was equal to that of everyone else in the room—though obviously for a different reason—so I felt they didn't know it was me. But I was so upset that my friend betrayed me. I kept asking myself, "Why would Keri use that information in that meeting, even after she promised not to?" If I admitted it, then everyone would know it was me. So much for making a good first impression. If I didn't admit it was me, then they would surely suspect it and hold it against me for not taking full responsibility.

I struggled with what to do; while it was only seconds that passed, it felt like days. It was as if I were seeing myself in a movie. I had two Jiminy Crickets on my shoulders. One was saying, You need to do the right thing. Admit it. Apologize and never let it happen again. The other one was saying, Keep your mouth shut. Don't be a fool. They will probably never know for sure who disclosed the e-mail and this will blow over. Besides, they think it was more than one board member. How could they know you were one of them? There will be another issue to fight about. Later you can try to fix this mess.

Judi: What did you end up doing?

Gael: I admitted it to everyone, right there and then. I apologized profusely and tried to explain the circumstances and the context under which the e-mail was shared, and hoped for the best.

Judi: Bravo! Great move. Very courageous. How did they take it?

Gael: Well, they were amazingly gracious. They appreciated the fact that I was willing to take quick and full responsibility for my actions. I even offered to quit the board. They had a long discussion in my presence. But at the end, they all agreed resignation was not necessary. They also acknowledged that the e-mail conversations were not marked confidential, and many of those arguments had already been made in public forums and were open for debate. Keri could have discovered the various positions of the board members in many ways, not just via the e-mail I had forwarded. Under the circumstances, they were wiling to give me another chance.

Judi: Did you ever talk to Keri about it?

Gael: You better believe I did. I immediately called
          her and shared everything that happened. Keri
          naturally apologized and explained that she had
          been receiving e-mails not just from me about
          the proposed legislation, but also from others.
          Keri thought that since there were others who
          had disclosed the same information without
          any assurances of confidentiality, it was safe to
          the share the information in an effort to more
          fairly describe the nature of the debate.

Judi: Did you forgive Keri?

Gael: Absolutely, I did. Keri and I had a long track
          record of mutual respect, support, and kept
          promises. I understood how and why she
          shared the information. But I didn't like it and
          I still wish to this day she hadn't shared that
          information with others. I'm a lot more careful
          now about e-mail.

What Lesson Did You Learn?

          Keri broke her promise to me by passing on
          the information. But I also realized that I had
          to take responsibility for my own actions. I was

the one who shared the information in the first place. I should have made it perfectly clear to Keri that this was a "pinky finger swear," which meant she could not share the information with anyone, for any reason and under any circumstances, ever.

Judi: How did this affect your relationship with the board members?

Gael: I felt as if I was a marked person bearing the scarlet letters "DO NOT TRUST THIS WOMAN." For the next few months, my relationships with all of them fluctuated from icy to cool, with occasional periods of lukewarm. And who could blame them? This situation had an impact on the vice president, the president, and other board members.

The vice president in particular always kept me at arm's length. She had been embarrassed in a meeting because of information I had leaked. The president had to deal with the turmoil this created among the board members, which I'm sure she was unhappy about.

Then new rules had to be put in place about e-mail etiquette because of my poor judgment and Keri's breach of confidence. I also think there were some board members who were never willing to trust me with any confidential information, and they would "accidentally" forget to include me in e-mail exchanges.

Judi: You know, Gael, what you did probably caused a few of those other secret e-mailers to breathe a sigh of relief. Too bad they didn't stand up and share some of the responsibility.

What Should a Big Girl Do?

Be careful about the information you share with others. Ask yourself, "Is it really necessary to share this information? In the big scheme of things, will it really make a difference?" Also realize that there is always the possibility that confidential information, or even secrets, will be shared with others. If you don't want something shared, then don't share it in the first place.

TAKE-HOME POINTS

• Think twice about the information you pass on to others. It may come back to bite you and your friend or colleague.

- If you do not want the shared information to get out, say so. Make sure you have a clear understanding of what "pinky finger swear" means to you and to others. And don't put it in an e-mail message, ever.

- If you get busted, take responsibility immediately, admit your mistake, apologize profusely, and never let it happen again. But don't automatically assume you are the guilty culprit. Oftentimes information gets leaked from multiple sources. It is not helpful to confess to crimes you did not commit.

What's Next?

Time for a look at "Not With My Ex!"

Rule Number Nine

Not with My Ex!

Gigi

Judi: One of my first rules with Teri was that we would never date each other's ex-boyfriends— or, later, our ex-husbands. How do you think that rule plays out in the workplace?

Gael: Judi, your rule "Not with My Ex" is a keeper. It definitely applies to the workplace. In fact, it happened to me with an ex-coworker who was my close friend and a coworker who became an ex-lover. As they say, breaking up is hard to do, but it's even harder to do if you breakup with someone from work. Some relationships will quickly recover, others may require more time and some may never recover at all. However it works itself out, it's usually easier to handle it privately and without everyone at work knowing about it. At the heart of any close relationship is loyalty, whether it's an intimate relationship, your best friend or a close colleague at work. We all want our friends and lovers to like us and to be loyal to us forever—even if we break up.

You can imagine how things get messy, and quickly too, when you're all working at the same place. You either have ex-friends or ex-lovers who eventually want to make new friends after the breakup, or, there will be other people who are just dying to be your ex-friend's or ex-lover's new friend! All of this is happening right in front of you and it can't be avoided. Oh my gosh, Judi, it's an invitation for hurt feelings and trouble. And we all know that hurt people, hurt people. I've experienced both situations—an ex-friend who left the company, an ex-lover who stayed at the company—with dramatically different results. Both stories have plenty of take-home messages for everyone

The Ex-Coworker

Once upon a time, a very close colleague and friend of mine, Gigi, decided to leave the organization without any notice or explanation—not even to me. Out of the blue, Gigi sent out an announcement of her departure. Her resignation was effective immediately. The announcement was very brief and caught everyone by surprise. Some people accepted the resignation without question. Others were naturally curious. Because I was one of her closest friends at work, some people called me to find out the true scoop. Other acquaintances called me with subtle questions about what happened or simply to express their concern.

Because I was genuinely surprised about the abrupt departure, it was easy for me to answer that I didn't know why Gigi left. I honestly told people that I had received the same message they did and suggested to everyone that they respect her privacy. "Let's all just hope good things happen, and when Gigi is ready to talk, she will," I said. My comments were always positive.

However, I wondered how this would really play itself out with other colleagues. Would everyone be as respectful and professional? Would mutual friends feel they would need to take sides with Gigi and the people left working at the organization? Would there be gossip and innuendos that she was asked to leave, or that she left as a result of a bad experience? Or would people just start to make things up in the absence any real information?

Quickly I discovered that, for the most part, I had the power to set the right tone. When I set a positive and professional tone, others followed suit. After a while it was also old news. Work went on.

Every once in a while I would hear from a mutual friend who traveled in the same circles as Gigi. Surprisingly, Gigi was not handling things in the way I expected. Gigi was instigating gossip and stirring the pot of innuendo. She was randomly calling mutual friends, asking what people were saying about her departure, and asking how people were surviving without her. Who was sitting in her office? How soon after she left was she replaced? Fortunately most of the friends I knew didn't want to engage in gossip and simply explained they were still friends with everyone who-worked there and planned to continue working with them for many reasons. Gigi's disruptive inquiries soon stopped. Our mutual friends were big. So being big helps others be big too!

The Ex-Boyfriend

The long-standing rule about not dating anyone at work is *so* true, but it is also a rule that is meant to be broken. The challenge for most single women is where to meet people, normal people, people who are not lunatics or criminals. The workplace can be a safe and convenient place, even a great place to meet your future husband or partner. I met my husband at work and our relationship has lasted twenty-three years. The office environment gives you a great opportunity to get to know someone from a safe distance and over a period of time. I could even meet his friends and learn about him as a professional. But before I married him, I broke up with him. Since he was personable, good looking and smart—at least some of the basic attributes women look for when searching for a partner—word spread very quickly that Jan was back on the market. Naïvely, I thought no one would date him because he was my ex. I was sadly mistaken.

Judi: Really, you thought that? Why did you care if someone else wanted to date him?

Gael: Women always care, even when they say they don't care. We care. Plus I still liked him. I really didn't think it was over … yet.

You see, Judi, I broke up with Jan on a Friday at 9 PM. By Monday morning, 10 AM, a woman, I had never met before, who worked for the company in the same building and on the same floor, brazenly walked into my office to confirm whether or not the rumor was true. She wanted to know if Jan and I had in fact broken up. When I told her yes, she proceeded to ask my permission to ask him out on a date.

For a moment I just stood there stunned. It never occurred to me that anyone from the company would date my ex-boyfriend, let alone ask for my permission. The little girl inside of me was ready to pull her hair and throw sand in her face. I felt like stomping my feet and throwing a tantrum. I wanted to say, "Who are you? Are you kidding me? Are you insane? Don't you know the rule that you never date another woman's ex, especially a woman that works at the same company?" Instead, I regained my composure and said, "Well, I really don't know what to say to you. That's not my decision to make. Jan will have to make that decision for himself." Then I just stood there, glaring at her, hoping she would get the hint that it was not okay with me.

In reality, what could I say? Jan and I did break up. He was fair game to any woman, including those who worked at the same company. I just had to wait and see what would happen next and hope that Jan would not go out with her. I really wanted to avoid the awkward moment of having to see him with another woman in the cafeteria or the parking lot.

The following week I had my answer. The same woman boldly walked into my office, but this time she was actually mad at me. In a harsh and raised voice, she said, "Why didn't you tell me Jan was still hung up on you? I invited him over to dinner at my house and all he talked about was you the entire night. He obviously still wants to date you. You put me in an embarrassing situation. You used me to get him to realize he wanted you back."

At this point, the little girl inside of me took over. I was now upset and I just reacted. I said, "Okay, that's enough. In the first place, I don't even know who you are. In the second place, what the heck were you thinking, asking Jan out just minutes after we broke up? You had no business asking him out. You never asked me if either one of us still had feelings for each other or if there was a possibility that we would get back together. Nor was it my responsibility to volunteer my feelings, hopes, or desires to you. Common sense would tell you we would likely get back together. And if you were going to ask him out, you should have waited much longer. So, lady, whatever hurt feelings you have now, you only have yourself to blame, not me. Don't come here asking for an apology from me or a shoulder to cry on. Those were self-inflicted injuries. Now, will you kindly leave?"

In retrospect, I wish I could have taken a bigger approach and remained calmer, but emotions took over. The good news, though, was that I never heard from her again. What's even more interesting is that when I shared this chapter with my husband, he had no recollection of the date ever happening in the first place. Go figure. I guess it all worked out for the best.

DISCUSSION

Judi: That was pretty brazen of her to charge in and ask your permission to date him, and then come back and blame you when the date didn't go well. You'd only been apart one weekend. I'm guessing that you were pretty broken up when she showed up in your office.

Gael: Well, I just wish I hadn't been in so much shock at the time all this happened. If I had my wits about me, I would have thought of something really smart and clever to say. But all I could do was give her the look and the silent treatment. However, I do give myself credit for those: If looks could kill I doubt if she would have made it to the elevator, which was just five feet away from our suite. Come to think of it, I never did see her again—ever. Not in the building, the elevator, the parking lot, or even the cafeteria.

Judi: Doesn't she get some credit for coming and asking your permission? That was very courteous, right? She wasn't your friend.

Gael: I think the rule you and Teri came up with is still true today. But it doesn't extend to every woman in the whole wide world or even the women that work in the same building. Obviously, the rule only goes so far. However, I'd add that you should be sensitive about dating a colleague's ex too. It would be wise to give it some time. There's always the strong likelihood that they will get back together, as Jan and I did.

TAKE-HOME MESSAGES

Judi: Okay, let's see what we can glean from this story that will help us all to be Bigger Girls when it comes to dealing with the end of relationships.

- Respect past relationships—yours and others.

- Don't get in the middle of struggling relationships or take sides.

- Be loyal to your friends. Loyalty matters. Loyalty and honesty will help you weather the storm.

- Give your friends time to be big and sort things out for themselves.

- Don't let relationships that have ended either at work or in your personal life interfere with your relationships with close friends or colleagues. Stay neutral and focused on your personal relationship with that person or workplace. Avoid the other stuff if you can.

- When it comes to intimate relationships, don't date your friend's ex-partner, ex-boyfriend, or ex-husband—ever.

- If you're thinking about dating a colleague's ex, at least wait until you are certain the relationship is over. (I added this one only because my husband said that otherwise Judi and I would be held personally liable for invalidating 80 percent of all successful relationships.)

What's Next?

Judi: On to the last chapter, "Lean on Me." Gael, you're up. Tell us about your best friend, Debbie.

Rule Number Ten

Lean on Me

Debbie

Debbie was one of the first real girlfriends that I met at work. She continues to be one of my best friends to this day. She was someone I could lean on, and she could lean on me; no exceptions. Debbie is for me what Teri is for Judi. While Debbie and I didn't have written rules, we had an understanding surprisingly similar to Judi and Teri's.

I remember meeting Debbie like it was yesterday. It was 1980. Debbie had recently been promoted as a legal secretary in the same law firm where I was working. One day, she walked into our suite with a big smile. She was making her rounds and introducing herself to everyone. She was my age with an engaging smile, a contagious laugh, and a twinkle in her eye. Within minutes I could tell we were going to be friends. I just liked the fact that she was smart, funny, and brave. I liked how she was so confident in herself that was willing to go out of her away to get to know people and find out how she could help them. Plus, I really liked the fact that she was short like me.

Before we knew it, we were going on breaks together. Breaks turned into lunch. Lunch turned into drinks after work. Drinks turned into dinners and special events over the weekend. Ultimately she became one of my closest confidants, one of my bridesmaids, and the godmother to my daughter. And along the way, we gave each other positive reinforcement and honest feedback. We learned from each other's work experiences and helped each other through some difficult challenges at work. We brought out the best in each other, and always thought the best of each other. She encouraged me to go to law school (at night while working full time). She was one of the friends that you could count on through the good and bad times. We accepted each other as a package—with all our quirks. I think the 95/5 rule first started with Debbie. We believed if we could be normal 95 percent of the time, it didn't matter if we were a royal pain in the neck the other 5 percent of the time. We figured now and then everyone was entitled to be cranky, quiet, or moody.

One of Debbie's first uncomfortable work experiences helped us both become Big Girls at the workplace—which was still male dominated at the time this happened, 1985. The situation involved a supervisor named Richard. Debbie was working as an executive assistant for one of the vice presidents of a large utility. She had been studying and preparing to become a planning assistant. During one of the company's reorganizations, Debbie was placed in that position. The planning department was 95 percent male. Most of the employees worked in the field, and the management ranks were populated with men who had made their way up the ladder through the traditional rank and file.

The men did not take well to Debbie joining their team with no prior field experience, although she had taken all the courses to prepare herself for the job and clearly knew the basics. They also went out of their way to make sure that she heard in advance that they didn't want her there, obviously hoping she would chicken out and rethink the assignment. But Debbie didn't give up. She showed up for work. On her first day, Richard immediately called her into his office and closed the door. With a tone dripping in condescension and intimidation, he said, "You know, Debbie, we actually work here in the planning department. It's not like the work you're used to doing back at headquarters with the vice presidents. Everyone who works here has earned their right to be here. They have worked in the field. They have worked their way up the ladder. This is hard work, little lady. You won't get the chance here to paint your nails all day long. And just so you don't complain we never told you, I just want you to know that this job isn't going to be easy for you. So don't blame me for how people will treat you here. It's just the way it is."

During this meeting, Debbie realized Richard was trying to bully her into quitting—to get her angry or to cry. Debbie just took a deep breath and calmly responded with her qualifications for the job, her work experience, and her work ethic. She explained she was prepared to do the job and also work hard. She meticulously walked Richard through her experience of earning her former position. She was never handed anything. She came from the school of hard knocks. Her attitude was always to do more than was asked of her. Debbie emphasized that she would be one of his hardest workers. She would learn quickly. She didn't mind the challenge and would welcome any assignment.

To Debbie's surprise, he just looked at her, trying to size her up. He then stood up and said, "All right, prove it." He handed her a stack of forty photographs and said, "By the end of this week I want you to tell me what each of these pieces of equipment are." And the meeting was over without a single welcoming gesture.

Debbie and I talked that night. It was one of the many Big Girl conversations we had over the course of our friendship. We believed Richard hadn't expected her to stand up for herself in such a calm and professional manner. His bullying tactics, which may have worked before, didn't work with this little lady. We focused our conversation on strategies and ways to be big. By the end of our conversation, Debbie had devised a plan in which she would learn everything there was to know about the department including the people, the job assignments, and every piece of equipment.

During her first week on the job, Debbie did just that. She identified her resources—where she would be able to get the information she needed and how she would learn—and even found someone who would be willing to help her and give her a fair chance at learning. Debbie leaned on Steve. Steve was a senior planner at the company who was well liked, respected and easily approachable. Steve just started out as a kind person. Though we did not fully appreciate the role he played at the time, he eventually became Debbie's mentor.

With her new friend Steve at her side, she went out into the field. She was introduced to people. She listened and learned from them. She studied the equipment and understood what their functions were. She learned what mattered to her colleagues.

By the end of the week, she went back to Richard's office with his stack of forty photos of insulators, lightning arresters, transformers, capacitor banks, and lots of other stuff that, to me, resembles much of what I find in the dark recesses of my son's closet. Debbie had not only figured out what they were but also explained how they worked and why they were needed. She completed his assignment as if it was no big deal at all. When I asked Debbie about how he reacted to their second meeting, she said he had that same look on his face, as if to say, "I didn't think you had it in you. And I'm pleasantly surprised."

From that point forward, things started to change between her and Richard. He started to be open to Debbie and she always treated him with respect. With each job assignment she completed, his respect for her grew. Debbie also never mentioned those early meetings to anyone outside of a close circle of friends and family. She never said a word about his rough treatment of her to anyone, although she easily could have gone to her former supervisor—a vice president at the company—and raised hell. That was not Debbie's style. She simply pledged to herself that she would ultimately earn his respect through her actions and become one of the best employees in the planning department. And she did.

As the years passed, Debbie came to consider Richard one of her closest friends. Richard ultimately recognized Debbie for her hard work, leadership, and excellent performance. None of this would have happened had Debbie reacted to the situation as anything other than a Big Girl.

DISCUSSION

Judi: Did you and Debbie talk further about this? Did you learn anything more about working with men? Couldn't Steve have thrown her under the bus, refused to help her?

Gael: Yes, of course. When Debbie and I later talked about her experience, I asked her why she asked Steve to help her and why she thought Steve, a senior male planner, was going to be willing to break ranks. Debbie explained that Steve seemed to be comfortable in his own skin and comfortable being around women. He didn't need to act macho in order to be macho. He seemed like a good guy with no ulterior motive, with a genuine interest in wanting to see his colleagues succeed, and it didn't matter if they were male or female.

What Lesson Did You Learn?

The conversation I had with Debbie concerning her trust in Steve turned out to be a valuable lesson for both of us about making new friends and finding colleagues who can be your mentor. The key was finding people who bring out the best in you—male or female.

What, If Any, Big Girl Rules Were Broken?

Judi: Can we say that that no Big Girl rules were broken in this story?

Gael: Definitely. None of the rules were broken by Debbie, although Richard wasn't very big at all. This is a story of being a Big Girl and finding other big girls at the workplace. Debbie didn't take things personally, she stayed big, she reached out to another Big Girl for help. She didn't gossip. She didn't get emotional. She gave people the benefit of the doubt. She kept her promises and she delivered. And she didn't give up her personal power.

Sadly, we also learned that there were more men willing to help women than women willing to help women. The women we were working with at that time had the rough edge that develops as a consequence of struggling single-handedly to navigate the good-old-boys club—a painful and difficult journey. They had the attitude that other women needed to do the same, that success should be earned without the support and help of other women.

What Solutions Did This Experience Bring to Light?

Fortunately, Debbie and I didn't give up. We looked everywhere for support, male and female. We learned the value of friendships, recognized it was okay to "lean on friends" and even recruited what we now recognize as mentors. In those days, we didn't have formal mentor programs, but there were people to "lean on" for help. Ultimately we learned to think of mentors this way: people with whom you are in regular contact, that you learn from and who enrich your life personally and professionally. Often mentors are individuals who simply care about the same things you do and likely share the same core philosophy and values. They may not think of themselves as being a mentor in the formal sense of the word. For Steve, he simply saw a coworker who needed help and he wanted to help. It didn't matter that the person needing help was female. It was his helpful nature that attracted Debbie to Steve, and allowed her to trust him and to lean on him.

In the same way Debbie developed a mentoring relationship with Steve, I had the good fortune of meeting Larry Cope early in my career. Larry was an experienced and senior attorney in the firm where I was working. He was someone who was willing to show me the ropes and help me figure out the steps to advance from legal secretary to paralegal, ultimately completing law school at night. Like Steve and Debbie, Larry and I started out as friends. I was eager, but struggling. He saw that I wanted to learn and wasn't afraid to ask questions. He was happy to step in with advice and guidance. These early relationships taught me that it was okay to lean on friends and coworkers, and that it was okay to seek out other mentors. Throughout my career I have found a number of mentors—both men and women.

TAKE-HOME MESSAGES

Judi: Gael, this is a very inspiring story. Could you summarize some of the take-home messages that could help us all be Big Girls?

- Look for people who like bringing the best out in others—whether male or female. A good friend is hard to find.

- Don't be afraid to lean on a friend for help, advice, or a sounding board. But most importantly, try to find someone who is willing to hold you accountable as a Big Girl.

- Find a colleague you can trust, one who is willing to mentor you in your professional career—even if it's a guy. Good guys are also hard to find but they are out there.

- Practice being wonderful to each other at least 95 percent of the time so that during the other 5% of the time, your friends will give you the benefit of the doubt.

- Be patient with others. Make room for others to find their way to being big.

- Always be big, especially when others are being mean to you. It will pay off at the end.

- Be a producer. When you are asked to perform a task, take it on, finish it, and bring it in on time and well done.

- In fact, do more than what you're asked to do. More often than not, people will reciprocate and go the extra mile for you.

- Consider making a mentoring relationship "official." Something magical can happen when you make it official. In our experience your mentor will take their role very seriously. The advice you get will be sound and will form the basis of a mutually beneficial and lasting learning exchange. We all have something to share with others and it could be the beginning of a long-term friendship.

What's Next?

Judi: Well, Gael, this has been fun, telling each other about our stories and the lessons we learned from them, and working together to get clear on the unspoken rules of the Big Girls Club. I can't believe we've finished. Don't we owe a lot to Jasmine, Wanda, Evelyn, Sally, Candy, Scarlett, Gina, Keri, Gigi, and Debbie? I'll kind of miss them—we've spent a lot of time with them as we put this book together. Seems like we are coming to the end. Do you want to lead us out of here?

Gael: Thanks, Judi. I do. Let's go ahead and move onto our conclusions.

Conclusion

Dear Friends,

Thank you for reading our book. Our goal in writing it was to share the hard and painful lessons both Judi and I have learned over our collective fifty years of working. We also wanted to celebrate the wonderful working relationship and friendship that has blossomed over the last ten years. Our short stories attempt to convey what worked and what didn't work for us.

It was also a personal journey for both of us. I wanted to share with my daughter, Samantha, as well as my son, Taylor, the things my mother couldn't tell me; both will work with many women and men throughout their careers. I want them to have a head start.

My mother clearly belonged to a different generation. She was eighteen years old when she married, nineteen when she gave birth to me, and twenty-seven when she divorced with three kids and no child support or alimony. She had to work two jobs to make ends meet. Work was not about friendships, it was about necessity. Developing relationships was the last thing on her mind. The workplace of my time and the workplace of her time are two different worlds.

Judi and I tried to imagine what the office of the future would be like if just a few more women adopted some of the rules of the Big Girls Club. Would it help shape the direction of the workplace in small but important ways? Would it make the workplace a better place for women and for men? Could it even turn two colleagues into best friends?

The feedback from the men in our lives has been very interesting. I think they were just as intrigued about this book as the women we talked to. Men wanted to know what women were thinking when they acted in certain ways. And they wanted in on the secrets of how women work with other women.

We recognize that relationships, whether at work or home, are not easy. They require hard work. But when you end up with lifelong friends like Judi and Teri, like Debbie and me, and now like Judi and me, it makes it all worthwhile.

Of course, relationships or friendships will be tested, over and over again. My relationship with Judi was tested right smack in the middle of writing this book. I'm not quite sure why we had our first major argument, but we did. Maybe we were tired, maybe we both started a diet when we shouldn't have, maybe we inadvertently hurt each other's feelings, or maybe—subconsciously—we were testing the true grit of this book, but one day emotions overran logic and we hit a wall. We couldn't talk it out or work it out. We needed a time-out, a breather from each other, and some time away from the book.

The good news is, after a twenty-four hour hiatus, we went back to the core principles of this book (which we've thought about, talked about, written about, agonized about, and even argued about for many years) and hit the reset button. We realized we still cared about each other, respected each other, and wanted to finish what we started. If we couldn't do that, then we had no business writing this book in the first place. And it was part of learning and growing. Life is about change, realizing that nothing stays the same. We grow, learn, adapt, and also change with change. I changed during the process of writing this book. Judi changed. Our relationship changed. It was supposed to change. Change is good.

Every generation of women will have their own rules for the workplace, whether known or unknown, written or unwritten. Hopefully each of us will learn from our mistakes, share lessons with others, and help others to become and continue to be Big Girls.

Why a Big Girls Club?

You've probably figured out by now that the Big Girls Club is about being a big person—doing things that need to be done, even when we don't want to. The Big Girls Club is about developing positive working relationships with women, and with men. The Big Girls Club is about making friends and finding and being mentors.

Judi and Teri were clearly ahead of their time by thinking and talking about rules of their friendship. Other relationships—like Debbie's and mine—had rules that were unspoken, but intuitively understood. After writing this book, Judi and I are confident that there are other Big Girls out there who have rules they live by even if they have never said them out loud or written them down.

We'd like to acknowledge some of the Big Girls who have been our friends and our mentors along the way. They know who they are. Some have been mentioned in this book. Some have not. The list is quite extensive and we want to honor their contributions to our lives. These women have touched our hearts and minds and have helped us be big.

Gael: Judi, would you add something here?

Judi: Thanks Gael, I will. Just a couple of additional thoughts.

Judi's Concluding Remarks

I love the reactions I get when I tell people one of our stories: "Hey, I know about that; it reminds me of my first job." "Did I ever tell you about *my* best friend?" "Here's a rule you should add to the list ..."

I think that's what I love most about the Big Girls Club. It's by sharing our stories that we get closer. We learn from one another. We remember that we need each other. Life is better with female friends. Today we spend more time at work, but less time face-to-face with each other. Some might say, "Why do we need to bother with being friends at all?" I'd say, "You spend more time at work than at home and you ask that question? Why would you not want to be friends?"

All those little spaces that we once used for building friendships are disappearing. Lunch hours are gone. Coffee breaks are nonexistent. We don't go into each other's offices. We don't meet in the company lounge. Instead, we e-mail, text-message, conference call, and webinar each other. We are busier than ever but we are not connecting with each other. And when we are disconnected, it's easy to make quick assumptions, take offense, and be small rather than big. I remember a group of women who were furious about an e-mail from a female colleague because of its tone. How can one correctly interpret *tone* in an e-mail, text message, or webinar?

Developing rules of the friendship for women in

the workplace isn't really so much about making a rule as it is about providing an opportunity to restart conversations. It helps create an atmosphere conducive to finding out what's important to everyone, discussing tender topics, sharing stories, and getting to know one another.

When Gael and I travel across the country and internationally, helping communities start their own Family Justice Centers, I always end the strategic planning portion by telling them about my friendship with Teri and Gael and some of our ground rules. Then we begin a conversation about what is important to their team—what rules of friendship do they want to put in place that will help them work together, stay the course, and provide a safe place to talk about and work through tough issues. As they come up with their own rules, they end up talking to each other about what's important to them, why they do the work they do, and what they need in order to feel valued and respected.

What Lessons Did We Learn Along the Way?

- Our own journey confirms our belief that it is all about relationships; women need each other, whether we are writing a book, running an organization, serving our country, or teaching in a preschool.

- Working together is co-creating. Gael and I could each have written this book alone, but by writing it together, like alchemy, we transformed our individual ideas into something greater. But if you think that was easy, you'd be wrong. Ideas can become very special. It's easy to forget that they don't belong to us to begin with; we just happened to stumble across that which already exists. How to work together, how to get past disagreements, through misunderstandings in order to stay the course and see the inherent value of the other, that's the trick. It is the purpose of the Big Girls Club.

- Sometimes the hardest part of addressing a problem is finding a way to bring it up. Having rules of friendship for the workplace opens the door to starting those conversations and helps us all to be Big Girls.

We Want to Hear from You!

Judi and I would love for you to be part of the Big Girls Club; we want you and your friends too. Share your copy of *The Big Girls Club*. Talk about it! Then contact us through our website, www.thebiggirlsclub. com. We are interested in your stories, your rules of friendship, your struggles and successes in the workplace with other women. We look forward to hearing from you.

And stay tuned for more books, like:

The Big Girls Club Workbook
The Big Girls Club—Stories from Around the World
The Big Girls Club—Working with Men

Hugs and kisses. Love you. Mean it.

Judi & Gael

A portion of the proceeds from the sale of this book are placed in a fund and used to promote peace, justice, and human rights.

About the Authors

Judi Adams is an internationally recognized strategic planner, coach, and trainer. For the past ten years her primary focus has been the Family Justice Center movement. She also has a broad professional background in organizational development, early childhood education, and community development. For the first ten years of her career, Judi was a single mother raising two boys (Jerry and Brian) while working for the Division of Psychiatry at Children's Hospital of Los Angeles on a nationally recognized child abuse treatment program. She has been honored for her work by numerous organizations, including the San Diego Urban League and the San Diego Domestic Violence Council. Additionally, Judi is an experienced motivational speaker on such subjects as "Ponies and Blankets: Finding and Keeping a Partner for Life," "Corduroy Bear: Helping Children Learn/Love to Read," and "The ABC's of Successful Parenting." She is a licensed marriage and family therapist, has a master's degree in education from the University of Southern California, and is the vice president of Adams & Adams Consulting and Training. Judi lives in San Diego with her husband, Carl. They have six grown children.

Gael Strack is the cofounder and chief executive officer of the Family Justice Center Alliance, which provides technical assistance to Family Justice Centers across the world. She served as a United States delegate to Poland and is currently providing technical assistance to Jordan and Bahrain through the State Department. Gael served as the director of the San Diego Family Justice Center, which was recognized as a model program by President Bush and was the inspiration for the president's Family Justice Center Initiative. Gael was a domestic violence prosecutor for many years at the San Diego City Attorney's Office. Prior to her employment with the city she worked for the San Diego County Counsel office, handling juvenile dependency matters. She began her legal career as a public defender in 1986. Gael has coauthored several books and written numerous articles on family violence prevention. She is currently an adjunct law professor for California Western School of Law. She has been honored with numerous awards, including San Diego Attorney of the Year in 2006.

Gael and Judi at the Arc de Triomphe, *Paris*

Printed in the United States
141930LV00001BA/1/P